TAKING CARE OF

Your Body

Sylvia Goulding

CHERRYTREE
BOOKS

Published in 2006 by The Evans Publishing Group
2A Portman Mansions
Chiltern Steet
London W1U 6NR

© 2005 The Brown Reference Group plc.

Printed in China

British Library Cataloguing in Publication Data

Goulding, Sylvia
  Taking care of your body. - (Healthy kids)
  1.Hygiene - Juvenile literature 2.Health - Juvenile
  literature
  I.Title
  613.4

ISBN-10 paperback:	1842343173
ISBN-13 paperback:	9781842343173
ISBN-10 hardback:	1842344110
ISBN-13 hardback:	9781842344118

PHOTOGRAPHIC CREDITS
Cover: **The Brown Reference Group plc**: Edward Allwright;
Corbis: (main image) Paul Barton; **Hemera Photo Objects**:
(bottom centre right)
Title page: **The Brown Reference Group plc**: Edward Allwright
BananaStock: 9, 13, 25, 29; **The Brown Reference Group plc**:
Edward Allwright 1, 4, 5, 6, 7, 8, 9, 10, 12, 15, 16. 17, 18, 20, 24, 28;
Hemera Photo Objects: 9, 10, 11,13, 15, 19, 21, 22, 26, 27;
RubberBall: 3; **Simon Farnhell**: 5, 6, 7, 11, 25.

FOR THE EVANS PUBLISHING GROUP

Editor: **Louise John**
Production: **Jenny Mulvanny**
Design: **D. R. ink**
Consultant: **Dr. Julia Dalton BM DCH**

FOR THE BROWN REFERENCE GROUP PLC

Art Editor: **Norma Martin**
Managing Editor: **Bridget Giles**

With thanks to models **India Celeste Aloysius, Daniel and Lydia Charles, Zac Evans, Isabella Farnhell, Georgia Gallant, Lydia O'Neill, Sam Thomson, Connor Thorpe, and Callum and Joshua Tolley**

Important note: Healthy Kids *encourages readers to actively pursue good health for life. All information in* Healthy Kids *is for educational purposes only. For specific and personal medical advice, diagnoses, treatment and exercise and diet advice, consult your doctor.*

Some words are shown in bold, **like this**. You can find out what they mean by looking in the glossary on page 30.

Contents

How to keep...
Your body clean

every day we touch millions of **germs**. Some germs are harmless, but others can make us ill. They can give us **infections**. Keeping clean can help to stop you catching some of these infections. Germs love warm, moist and dirty places. Keep yourself clean, and germs won't stand a chance. If you're dirty or sweaty after doing sport, always have a bath or a shower.

◄ *Wash your hands with a bar of soap and warm water. The soap takes off the dirt. It also makes your hands smell nice.*

Or try this...

Wash your hands after...
- going to the toilet
- gardening or playing outside
- sneezing or coughing

Just amazing!

No flannel needed...
- It's easy for a giraffe to clean its ears. Its tongue is 50 centimetres long so it can reach hidden places.

Clean hair and scalp

▶ *If you catch head lice, use a comb to remove them.*

Healthy hair

Your **scalp** makes oils that protect your hair. When you use shampoo, you wash out the dirt. Don't wash your hair too often though, or you'll wash out the oils that keep it healthy, too.

Shiny hair

What you eat affects your hair. If your hair looks lifeless, check your diet. For healthy hair eat wholemeal foods, eggs, oily fish like tuna and salmon, carrots and green vegetables.

Fighting head lice

Head lice pass from person to person. They're irritating but not dangerous. To get rid of them, you can buy special shampoo from the chemist. Put the shampoo on your hair, then comb the lice out. Repeat until all the lice are gone.

hair grows faster in summer

you have about 100,000 hairs

each year hair grows about 12 cm

▶ *Shampoo and some hair gels can make Afro hair dry. Try petroleum jelly to style and protect.*

Furry and feathery friends

It's important to keep clean around animals, too. Don't let them lick your face and always wash your hands after touching pets.

Caring for your...
Hands and feet

feet sweat in trainers and can get smelly. In changing rooms and swimming pools you can sometimes catch infections. **Athlete's foot** makes the skin between your toes itchy. Always wash and dry your feet well. Care for your hands, too. Keep them warm and wash them properly (read about it on page 4).

◀ *Keep your toenails short so you don't hurt your other toes. Cut them straight across the top.*

wash sweaty feet?

Just amazing!

Amazing feet...
- Horses walk on tiptoe, called a hoof.
- We walk around 8,000 steps each day.
- A quarter of our bones are in our feet.

Nicer nails...

Cutting your nails

Shape your fingernails into a gentle curve. Use special nail scissors and a fine nail file.

Chewing nails

Some children bite their nails because they are nervous. Talking about your worries is much better.

Broken and split nails

If your nails break or split, soak them in water. Then rub in a moisturising cream. Eat more cheese and drink more milk. These foods contain **calcium**, which makes your nails strong.

▲ *Wear gloves to keep your hands warm in cold weather.*

wear shoes that fit well

In Finland, Santa brings naughty children a bag of toenail clippings instead of toys!

Just amazing!

The longest thumbnails...

A man in India grew the thumbnail of his left hand to a record length. The nail measured 142cm!

Amazing fingernails...

A doctor can tell from your nails if you are ill. For example, broken nails and white spots mean that you're not eating well.

dry between the toes

◀ Wind, weather and heating can dry your skin. Use skin cream.

In touch with...
Your skin

Your skin is an amazing 'wrapper' around your body. It keeps water and dirt out and keeps everything safe inside your body. Skin sweats to keep you cool when it's hot.

It produces goosebumps to keep you warm. If you scrape your knee, it makes a **scab** and heals over. Your skin is made up of **cells**. Every day, we shed hundreds of dead cells and grow new ones.

Or try this...

Natural skin care...
● Before showering, brush your skin with a soft brush. Start at your feet and work up. This brushes away dead skin cells.

Safety first!

Remember...
● The sun is strong even when it's hazy.
● Winter sun can burn you, too.
● Sun is extra strong near water or snow.

Sun and skin

Is the sun good for me?
Sun makes us healthy and happy. But the sun's rays are strong and can be dangerous. Make sure your skin never burns.

How long can I be in the sun?
You should only stay in direct sun for short periods of time. Always stay out of the midday sun, from 12.00 to 3:00 p.m.

What should I wear?
In the sun, wear a good sunhat. Wear loose-fitting cotton clothes and always wear plenty of high factor sun cream!

◄ *Pale, freckled skin – stay mainly in the shade. Use a cream with factor 30–40.*

◄ *Light brown skin – you can stay for short periods of time but you still need to use a factor 15–20.*

◄ *Darker skin – you can stay in the sun a little longer, but you still need to use a factor 15.*

▶ *Suncream is fun and looks cool!*

If you do get sunburned...
- Apply calamine lotion to the burn.
- Cover up with loose clothing.
- If the burn is severe, see a doctor.

Looking after...
Your eyes

your eyes are your windows to the world. They make you see people and things around you. But sometimes things go wrong. What you see can become blurry and not in **focus**. Regular visits to the **optician** for eye tests are a good idea. In most cases a pair of glasses will help you see better.

◀ *Reading lots should not affect your eyes, but always make sure you read in good light.*

Don't try this...

What makes your eyes red and tired...
● hours staring at the television or the computer screen
● lots of smoke or dust in the air

Safety first!

Bright sunshine...
● ...can be harmful to your eyes. Wear sunglasses to protect them, especially at the seaside or in the snow.

Problem eyes

If you are shortsighted...
You can see things clearly close up. Everything far away is blurred. Glasses can help you to see better.

If you are longsighted...
You can see faraway things, but what's in front of you is all fuzzy. Glasses can help you to see better.

If you are colour blind...
Few colour-blind people see the world in black and white. They just find it hard to see certain colours – usually red, blue or green. In this circle some won't be able to see a number.

If you have a squint...
One eye looks in a different direction from the other.

Carrots and other orange foods are great for your eyes. They can help you to see better at night!

Eat orange-coloured fruit and vegetables...
● Apricots, mangoes, melons, oranges and carrots are all rich in vitamin A. It helps you see well, especially in the dark.

▶ *Glasses help you to see better and they can also be fun!*

Taking care of...
Your ears

your ears do two different jobs: they help you hear and they give you balance. They give you pleasure when you listen to music and they help you back on your feet when you're dizzy after a funfair ride. Be careful though – loud noise can damage your ears so badly that you won't be able to hear properly when you get older.

▶ *Enjoy your favourite music, but keep the volume down low so you don't damage your ears – or annoy your parents!*

Safety first!

To stop ears popping on a plane...
...suck on a boiled sweet and swallow lots. Yawn or hold your nose and swallow until you can hear properly again.

There's something in my ear...
If there is something stuck in your ear, it's best not to try to get it out yourself. Go to visit the doctor and they will help.

Ear facts

Ear problems

Earache

If your ear is swollen, red or painful, tell your doctor. You might have an infection. The doctor may prescribe some medicine. He or she will tell you what you should and shouldn't do to help your ear to get better.

Ear wax

Everyone has small amounts of ear wax. It builds up inside your ear and then drops out. If yours doesn't, put a couple of drops of olive oil in your ear every night to soften the wax. If you still have problems after a week or so, go to see the doctor.

▶ *Don't put anything inside your ears, not even cotton buds.*

elephants use their ears as fans

the smallest bone is in the ear

Just amazing!

Name that tune...

Babies can hear music even before they are born. And they can tell when they hear the same tune again!

an earache can make you feel dizzy

Looking after...
Your mouth

When you first meet people, give them a warm smile, with two rows of healthy, gleaming white teeth. Brush your teeth thoroughly, from the **gums** to the tips. If you don't brush properly, germs collect on and around your teeth and near your gums. This is called **plaque**. It can rot your teeth and eventually make them fall out.

◄ *Brush your teeth twice a day and after meals. Thoroughly clean the front and back of each tooth. Brush the tops of your teeth, too.*

Or try this...

Care for your lips...
Your lips may crack in cold weather and in the sun. Use a sunblock and keep lips moist with a lipsalve.

Safety first!

Stop plaque...
- Brush twice a day and after meals.
- Floss thoroughly between your teeth.
- Visit your dentist at least twice a year.

Seeing the dentist

Toothache

Do your teeth feel painful when you eat or drink something hot, cold or very sweet? It can be a sign of **tooth decay**. The dentist might need to give you a filling.

Gum disease

If you don't brush well, your gums can get sore and infected. They will bleed when you brush. The dentist will show you how to brush properly.

Crooked teeth

If your teeth are crooked, the **orthodontist** may give you dental braces to wear. They can straighten your teeth over a period of time.

▲ *An orthodontist takes a mould of your teeth before fitting you with dental braces.*

▼ *Sweets are full of sugar, which rots your teeth. Brush thoroughly after eating them. Or try not to eat them at all!*

Keep your gums healthy...

- Gently brush your gums and your teeth.
- Use a new brush every three months.
- Don't eat sweets.

Feeding...
Your body

eating healthy food is important. It stops you getting ill. It gives you strong bones and makes you grow. Eating the right food can even make you clever and look good. You can think better if you eat a good breakfast. Your hair grows shiny, and your nails don't break. Don't snack on junk food – it makes you tired, unfit and overweight.

◀ *Healthy meal – colourful vegetables and salad, grilled chicken and fresh orange juice.*

▶ *Unhealthy meal – burger and chips, soft white roll, tomato sauce, mayonnaise and a fizzy drink.*

Do eat this...

Try to eat plenty of these foods...
- fruit and vegetables: Chew on fresh or dried fruits instead of snack bars. Pile salad and vegetables high on your plate.
- wholemeal food and **legumes –** brown rice, lentils, peas
- vegetable oils – Brazil nuts, olives
- Drink fresh fruit juice and water.

What you need...

Food facts

Starchy food
Eat plenty of wholemeal bread, rice, pasta and potatoes.

Fruits and vegetables
Eat at least five portions a day. Choose foods of different colours.

Proteins
Eat two servings a day of meat, fish, milk, cheese or legumes like peas and lentils.

eat lots of fruit and vegetables

Fats
Eat as little fatty food as you can. Avoid animal fats. Choose healthy fats, in nuts, olives and oily fish.

eat wholegrain foods

Don't eat this...

Try not to eat a lot of...
- fatty and fried food – burgers, chips, hot dogs, chicken nuggets, fishfingers
- snack foods – crisps, popcorn

- sugary food – cakes, biscuits, chocolate
- sauces – mayonnaise, ketchup
- sugary drinks – fizzy drinks, flavoured water, fruit drinks without real fruit

avoid fat and sugar

17

Get active for life

to stay healthy you need to get active. If you don't like school sports, there are lots of other things you can do. Strong muscles can protect you from injury and broken bones. Speed and staying power keep your lungs and heart fit. Being active helps you think better. It also makes you look good. Here are lots of great ideas for what to do.

Exercising your body

Fitness facts

Super strong muscles
Lie on your back and air-bicycle. Run up and down stairs. Hop on one leg and squat up and down.

Sensational speed
Race your friends in the garden, across the swimming pool, on a skateboard, a bike or up a hill. Or race against yourself.

◀ When you're cycling or skateboarding, always wear a helmet and knee pads.

Stunning stamina
If you get out of breath easily, you may need to improve your fitness. Try swimming, running or dancing. Don't go up in the lift – walk up the stairs.

Fabulously flexible
Stay flexible. Stretch up on tiptoes. Kick box the air. Bend your body forwards, backwards and sideways. Practise keeping up a hula hoop.

do at least 20 minutes each day

be active every day

vary your activities

Or try this...

Exercising your mind...
● Set up a crossword tournament.
● Play a memory game – remember as many capital cities as you can.

● Get creative – try dancing, singing, writing stories or painting.
● Learn to play thinking games like chess.
● Read a play and act out different roles.

▼ Don't hurt your back when you lift a heavy object. Squat and bend your knees. Keep your back straight.

How to avoid...
Hurting yourself

there are many ways to hurt yourself. You could stumble and fall, or you could cut yourself. **Injuries** can happen anywhere, even when you're playing or doing sports. If you know what to watch out for, you can help to avoid accidents. There are two ways to protect yourself: (**1**) wear the right protective clothing like helmets and padding; (**2**) get active so your bones and muscles are strong enough to protect you.

Safety first!

When you're playing outside...
● Wear a helmet and kneepads when you are cycling or skateboarding.
● Follow the rules in every sport you do.

In the UK, children get more sports injuries from playing football than any other sport!

Be careful...

In the house

Be careful around the cooker and don't knock any pots or pans over. Put your toys away so that you don't trip over them. Don't kick balls around the house. You could break something or hurt yourself badly.

In the garden

Many plants are poisonous. Don't touch them unless an adult has told you it's safe. Be especially careful near water. Don't play in sheds or with garden tools. They cause many injuries.

▼ *If you cut yourself, get help. A clean wound heals faster.*

● Be very careful in traffic. Don't run into the road after balls or pets.
● If you're playing in the water, make sure a responsible adult is watching you.

▶ *Never, ever play with chemicals or electrical equipment.*

Staying away from...
Danger

Life is fun – most of the time. But you need to keep away from certain things. Don't drink alcohol or smoke. They can make you very ill. Don't let your friends push you into drinking or smoking. Be tough and say 'no'. Don't let other people upset you. If they want to do something to you that you don't like, walk away. Get help. And never, ever take any **drugs**!

◀ *Stay away from the medicine cabinet. Never take any medicines unless your parents or a doctor have told you to.*

Don't ever try this...

Dangerous people...
● Your body is yours alone. Don't ever agree to do something you don't want to do, no matter how persuasive someone is.

● Don't ever walk off or drive away with anyone you don't know.
● Don't ever agree to meet up with anyone you meet on the Internet.

Don't smoke

Smoking can kill...
Smoking gives you bad breath. It stains your teeth. It costs lots of money and it can kill you. Cigarettes have two bad ingredients: **nicotine** and **tar**. Nicotine makes you **addicted** so that you always want more. Tar can cause clogged arteries, heart disease, strokes and lung cancer.

Don't drink alcohol

Alcohol can kill...
Even if your friends sometimes try alcohol, just say 'no'. Alcohol gives you bad breath and it makes you behave oddly or fall over. If you drink too much, you feel ill. Alcohol can make you addicted. It can make you worried and unhappy. It can give you liver disease, a stroke, heart disease and sometimes even cancer.

Safety first!

What to do in an emergency...
- Call 999 for police, fire or ambulance.
- Tell the operator exactly what's wrong.
- Tell him or her where you are.
- Stay where you are so that you can be easily found.
- Try to keep calm.
- Help if you can.

Body and mind at ease

Staying healthy and fit is a good start for a healthy, happy mind. If you feel too much **stress**, you can get moody or angry. You might snap at friends, cry a lot or have bad dreams. Stress can even make you ill. Learn to unwind. There are many ways to do this. If you have a serious problem, seek help.

◄ *Join a class and learn* **yoga** *for children. It unwinds body and mind.*

get a good night's sleep

Or try this...

You can relax by...
- doing some exercise
- having a warm bubble bath
- stroking your cat or dog
- tidying up your bedroom
- doing some gardening
- going for a walk in the countryside
- visiting friends and chatting with them

▲ *Music can help you relax. Sit back and listen to your favourite tunes. Or sing along as loud as you can!*

eat healthy food

▶ *Drawing is a quick way to get rid of a bad mood. Or read a funny book that you enjoy.*

A stressful life...

School problems

Worried about exams? Plan your work to help you pass. Not getting on with other children? Ask a teacher for help.

Family problems

Stressed because your parents argue or are getting divorced? Ask a teacher for help.

Safety first!

Help with big problems...

● Speak to a teacher or your parents if you are being bullied by other children.

● See a doctor if you're very unhappy.

● If you'd rather talk about your problems to someone who doesn't know you, you can call ChildLine on 0800 1111 for some free and friendly help and advice.

do some exercise

Health people...
Caring for you

hundreds of people work all day every day to make sure that you will not get ill. And if you do feel unwell, they are there to help. They can check all parts of your body, inside and out. And they'll give you the best medicine and treatment to make you feel better again quickly.

◄ *If you're ill you may have to stay in hospital. Nurses will take your temperature if you have a fever. Doctors will check you every day.*

Did you know?

Other health workers...

Many people work in health. Some are **specialists**. They concentrate on just one part of your health.

There are heart specialists, blood specialists and bone specialists. Some doctors are specialists just for children's diseases.

Who's who?

Doctors
They help you get better when you are ill. And they can give you **vaccinations** to stop you catching certain diseases.

School nurses
Some schools have a school nurse. They watch your health at school.

Opticians
They treat you for eye problems and order glasses.

Dentists
They check and treat your teeth.

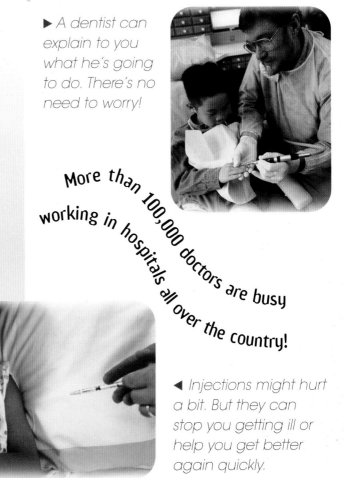

► *A dentist can explain to you what he's going to do. There's no need to worry!*

More than 100,000 doctors are busy working in hospitals all over the country!

◄ *Injections might hurt a bit. But they can stop you getting ill or help you get better again quickly.*

Just amazing!

● The doctor may examine you to find what's wrong. He may check your blood or urine for diseases. Or he may take an **X-ray** of the inside of your body.

Live a long and healthy life...
● A French woman, Jeanne Calment, was one of the oldest women ever. She died when she was 122 years old!

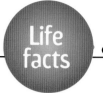

Take care of your body for...
A happy life

looking after your body is not hard. Just follow the ideas in this book: eat well, sleep well, keep yourself clean and get lots of exercise. The rewards come straight away. You'll stay healthy. You'll look good and feel good. You'll have bundles of energy to work and play.

◄ Healthy childen have lots of fun playing together.

sleep well
2

Safety first!

Tell your doctor if...
- You don't feel well a lot of the time.
- You suffer from aches and pains and don't know why.

Tell the school nurse if...
- You gain or lose a lot of weight.
- You've hurt yourself at school.
- You have any health questions.

Test yourself

1. Which of these sentences is true?

A You should wash your hands at least
once every hour during the day.

B You should wash your hands
after you've been to the toilet.

C You should wash your hands
after you've stroked a pet.

2. To be fit and healthy you need:

A three hours at the gym every day

B 20 minutes of activity a day

C half an hour of sports a month

3. Which are good foods to eat?

A plenty of fruits and vegetables
of different colours

B burgers, chips, hot dogs, fizzy drinks

C wholemeal bread, brown rice,
pasta and potatoes

**4. If you're stressed
you should...**

A Pull yourself together and
stop moaning all the time.

B Try something relaxing, like
yoga or going for a walk.

C Go to a hospital for an operation.

**5. Match these jobs to what
they look after:**

A dentist   a eyes

B optician   b vaccinations

C doctor   c teeth

ANSWERS: 1B and C, 2B, 3A and C,
4B, 5: Ac, Ba, and Cb.

keep clean 1

get active 3

Tell your parents if...
- You get so worried you can't sleep.
- You've got problems with your friends.
- You're really happy!

◄ *Healthy
children work
hard and
get good
marks at
school.*

Glossary

What does it mean ?

addicted: If you cannot stop taking something you are addicted to it.

athlete's foot: An infection that makes the skin between the toes sore and itchy.

calcium: Calcium makes healthy teeth and bones. Milk and cheese contain calcium.

cell: The smallest building block in our body. Your body contains billions of cells.

drugs: Illegal chemicals that are addictive.

focus: Something is in focus if you can see it clearly.

germs: Very tiny living things that can make you ill. Bacteria and viruses are germs.

gums: The firm pink flesh around teeth.

infections: Diseases caused by germs.

injury: Damage or harm.

legumes: Beans, lentils and peas.

nicotine: A dangerous chemical in tobacco. It is addictive.

optician: A specialist who checks your eyesight and orders glasses if you need them.

orthodontist: A dentist who improves crooked teeth.

plaque: A sticky layer of food and bacteria on the surface of teeth.

scab: Dried blood that hardens and covers a cut or sore. Scabs help wounds heal.

scalp: The skin on top of your head.

specialists: People who learn more about one part of health. They become experts.

stress: A lot of worry, or great pressure.

tar: A dangerous chemical in tobacco. Tar damages lungs, with which you breathe.

tooth decay: A disease that rots your teeth.

vaccination: An injection that stops you getting ill.

X-ray: An image that sees through your skin.

yoga: Exercises for body and mind. They help you relax all over.

To find out more...

...check out these books:

● Gaff, Jackie. Cherrytree Books, 2005.
Why Must I...Take Exercise?
Why Must I...Wash My Hands?
Why Must I...Brush My Teeth?

Why Must I...Eat Healthy Food?
● Ganeri, Anita. Evans Brothers, 2006.
The 'How My Body Works' series. Titles: Moving, Breathing, Senses, Brain, Blood and Eating.

To find out more...

...check out these websites

● www.jointheactivaters.org.uk/
Children's website promoting healthy eating and physical activity.

● www.childrenfirst.nhs.uk/
Advice for children on all aspects of general health.

● www.itsnotyourfault.org/
Practical advice for children going though a family break-up.

● www.keepkidshealthy.com/welcome/
commonproblems/sportsinjuries.html

● www.childline.org.uk

● www.kidscape.org.uk/
Children's website dedicated to the prevention of bullying and abuse.

● www.givingupsmoking.co.uk
/Young_people__smoking/
Information for young people about giving up smoking.

● Waters, Fiona. *What About Health?: Drugs*. Hodder Wayland, 2004.
● Ballard, Carol. *Keeping Healthy: Harmful Substances*. Hodder Wayland, 2004.

● Sanders, Bruce. *Talking About: Bullying*. Franklin Watts, 2003.
● *Look After Yourself* KS2 CD Rom. Evans Publishing Group, 2006.

Index
Which page is it on?